# YELLOW ARROW

Vol. VII, No. 2
Fall 2022
*Peregrine*

# Yellow Arrow Journal

Creative nonfiction, poetry, and cover art by writers/
artists that identify as women

Vol. VII, No. 2
Fall 2022
*Peregrine*


## Editor-in-Chief
Kapua Iao

## Guest Editor
Raychelle Heath

## Editorial Associates
Jackie Alvarez-Hernandez, Siobhan McKenna,
Beck Snyder, and Rachel Vinyard

## Contributors
Rina Malagayo Alluri, Elizabeth Bowden-David,
Rebecca Brock, Wren Donovan, Elaine Elinson,
Patricia Falkenburg, Jen Gayda Gupta, Christine C. Hsu,
Blaise Allysen Kearsley, Amanda Kooser, Christina Lengyel,
Diann Leo-Omine, Kari Ann Martindale, Oanh Nguyen,
Tamiko Nimura, Ray Oldham, Maria S. Picone,
Janet M. Powers, Leticia Priebe Rocha, Kathryn Reese,
Laura Rockhold, Ellen Skilton, and Hana Worku

## Cover Art
Daryle Newman

YELLOW ARROW
PUBLISHING

PO Box 102, Baltimore, MD 21057
info@yellowarrowpublishing.com

**Yellow Arrow Journal - Peregrine**
Copyright © 2022 by Yellow Arrow Publishing
All rights reserved.

ISBN (paperback): 979-8-9850704-5-3
ISSN (print): 2688-3015
ISSN (online): 2688-3023

Cover art by Daryle Newman (Instagram @daryle_shefloats).
Cover and interior design by Yellow Arrow Publishing.
For more information, see yellowarrowpublishing.com.

# LICHEN BLOOMS
## Laura Rockhold

I'm happy to slow down,
     to see the lichen blooms'
aging beauty. Mille-feuille petals
     of pale mint, color the scent
of vetiver on skin. Leaflets of melon-
     speckled blue, color light
as kindness. Blurring what it is to be two,
     fungus and algae in symbiotic
reciprocity. A whole us. In Mni Sota Makoce,
     "land where the waters are so clear
they reflect the clouds," I have been
     the water. And you,
the clouds. Blooming somehow
     for a coat of brilliance.
Today will be different tomorrow.
     I can tell
when you're feeling me—
     you move in a little closer,
twirl me around to see—
     victory's still alive in me, dancing,
you know,
     I gave up my name
(a few times)
     before I claimed it.

# Table of Contents

*Dear Readers,*

I grew up in a small town in South Carolina. From a young age, I was in love with what words could do. I grew up loving stories—reading them, listening to them, and eventually writing them. There are stories that my family loves to tell, like the time I wanted to show my parents' guests how well I could use my potty. And there are stories that I love to tell, like the time I got to see Prince in concert. When I first started writing, I remixed my favorite stories. Taking tales like Aladdin and Greek myths and giving them my own spin.

I first came to poetry through rhymed and metered children's verse about gardens and animals. I then moved on to Emily Dickinson, whose work I still love. But it wasn't until I began to read Lucille Clifton, Nikki Giovanni, and Alice Walker that the words I saw on the page sounded like me and the people around me. It was music that I could understand, and that invited me to participate. I wanted to show up on the page like they did. As much as I wanted that, my first poems were pretty terrible. It took a while to shake the idea that poems had to rhyme or brood. But little by little, I began to shake off what I thought poetry was supposed to sound like and began finding my stride. This was despite the outside voices telling me that I needed to explain/change/fix my work so that it could be understood.

Eventually I became an English teacher. I was tasked with teaching my students grammar and syntax. And in the classroom, they got the unaccented English of textbooks and scholarly papers. And I taught them how to wield that language—where to put commas, how to correctly spell a word, proper conjugation, etc. These were the tools that they needed to pass the class, and in many ways to pass in life.

There was a time when I felt like my poetry also had to sound like my buttoned-up teacher voice. I'm not sure why that idea latched to my brain. I knew there were other ways to make the page sing; I read writers who let their language be free. But shaking those highly ingrained lessons of what was "correct" was hard. Eventually I did shake them off and began to let my language bloom however it needed to. Sometimes the words showed up in the most flowery of ways, sometimes they had a southern sway like my aunties, and sometimes the words weren't in English at all. And when I eventually began to teach creative writing, I got to share that freedom with my students. I got to show them how we writers can meet our page as creatives and allow our words to be free. Just like when I meet my aunt on her wraparound porch or my grandpa reclining in his La-Z-Boy; my tongue can relax, the south can come out, my specific family tongue can unfold.

Over the years I have had the pleasure of being in community with writers that speak many languages, and for some, English isn't their first language. And it got me thinking about what is lost when one language becomes the standard and what concessions are made on the page when we default to that language. And even deeper, what happens when we put further demands on that one language—that it must be structured a certain way to be valid. How does that change how the page sings? These were the thoughts moving through me as I brainstormed themes for *Yellow Arrow Journal*, Vol. VII, No. 2.

I went through quite a few theme ideas for this issue, but ultimately **PEREGRINE** felt right. I remember learning about peregrine falcons in school—how they traveled, how they knew home. And in so many ways, the community of writers I know and love are finding and sharing home in the way they use words. As a traveler myself, finding home in places of welcome, the word peregrine feels like it also applies to me, and to this broader human experience that we are all traveling through in one way or another.

What you will find in these pages are writers that are exploring their own journeys with language and home. Sometimes it is the language of their parents that wasn't passed down, sometimes it is language that they are just now in a place to own. Other times it is the language of nature that is communicating with them or the language of a body that they are getting to know.

Throughout these explorations our writers find ways to reclaim their language and their place. Hopefully the work you find here will illuminate how you, too, can reclaim a language and place that feels authentic, like you, like home. Thank you, gracias, and kommol tata for supporting the work we do.


*Sincerely,*

Raychelle Heath
Guest Editor

# PEREGRINE

# *Lost In*
## Leticia Priebe Rocha

Though unquestionably it was vermin,
I couldn't do it, run over
the rat scurrying across the street. A slice of me
wanted to hit the gas. Driving away from
the averted casualty, I searched
to name that slice. To run over
in Portuguese is atropelar, a harsh utterance
efficient in its violence. There is no way to say I miss you
in Portuguese, there is only saudade—
an **it** that you possess for something, someone.
Finding photographs of streets I once walked,
taken by my mother years before
my birth. Googling the city of my first
childhood, the top result, a bridge built two years after
my flight. Losing my love
for Pizza Hut following our last meal
as a family before my father left. Saudade.
A horrible man once told me, guaranteed
that atheists are fools for every person will someday
be brought to their knees by something
so dire they will want God to be real. Want,
not need. I didn't understand that, didn't understand
that a want could be greater than a need, that I could
become want. Driving past a tree, in
the curved ridges of its trunk I saw the Mother Mary,
her leaves screaming in the wind—saudade.
A bowling ball of longing wedged in the middle
of my chest, minuscule cracks pushed
into ribs, lungs flattening, heart lopsided, beating
for skies that we will never see.

# *Watching Mountains*
## Rebecca Brock

Even though the room faces west,
the sunset plays the mountains,
and I see how long a day can be,
well spent, standing still
and held there—two white birds
flicker with sunlight—the sky
as if it might snow, that mist of fog,
but then a late gasp of wide blue.
I am in the city at the base
of those mountains, a stretch
of the Rockies, caught between
time zones, between here
and back again, I stand
at a hotel window
naming want—those hills,
I mean, to be in them—
what is time to a mountain,
beyond season, beyond sun—
the gathering of rain—
a mountain lion's call,
the stone ringing with light
like a name that's learned to speak
for itself—what is it to feel yourself unmoving?
Any shift would rumble
like bone crack
like cadence, the fall of rock
or impact—they rest
the way the sea sways,
that wash of crash and pull.

There is no pulse
in a mountain—just the fact
of its being—as if to say here,
just here—a reminder
of what was, what is,
and someday immeasurable
what will no more be.

# *one day i'll pinch off the dead leaves and call this body a home*
### Ray Oldham

i named my first plant Horatio so that he couldn't die,
but i forgot a fate to survive didn't mean a promise
to never change. little ivy leaves grow
and brown and fall and sprout anew
in a way much more recognizable than my own.
one day i'll self-prune and rejoice
in my new limbs as readily and easily as i wiped the spider mites
from every leaf on his little struggling body,
without judgment, without pause.
one day i won't mind the dirt.
and i thought, once, as a child, it could be possible to go home,
but then the sun never stopped setting
and that flower in my neighbor's yard bloomed and died.
the things i thought were set in stone
were the things that'd always change. one day i'll learn
to accept the shifting of the shadows
across my bedroom wall. one day i'll know
the passing of time as more than just another thing passing me by,
more than a thing of which to be terrified.
the weather tries to teach me different, while the seasons try
to ease my mind, but i still too often look at the evening sky and decide
the shade of orange isn't familiar enough for comfort.
one day i'll sit in the grass
and it won't feel like an ocean; it'll feel like life, like living,
present and prescient, like the next thirty years
on the tip of my tongue, permanently, perfectly unpredictable
in taste; it'll feel like grass.
and i could rip up the dewy green blades
to make a pile tall enough to take me
where the sun stops moving,

but then i could never again see the sky reflected
in my best friends' eyes. one day i'll shed a tear
over something new rather than something gone.
one day i'll stop leaving the light on.
and when i look at Horatio and think it might be possible
to settle into change,
the thought of it all finally doesn't feel
so far away. one day i'll love the way my body has grown into this house,
the way my future has grown into something i'm forever trying
to recognize. one day
i'll pinch off the dead leaves and it'll feel like a sunrise.

# *Handsome*
## Amanda Kooser

Today, passing by the silver of the bathroom mirror, I see an angularity to my face, and, for a moment, I think myself handsome.

I am grateful for a world, damaged and dangerous though it can be, that is waking up to find that gender identities and expressions aren't simple things. As I celebrate the movement forward, I also look back to my past and wonder about who I might have been in light of what I know now.

When I was perhaps four or five, our family bustled around the Victorian house in Galesburg, Illinois, where I grew up. My mother adjusted the sleeves of her dress, something flowing, suggestive of the 1960s and Northern California and cool bay breezes. We were going to a wedding. I sat on the side of her bed, kicking my legs and wailing, fists like pendulums beating against the sheets as she held up my little blue dress with the white flowers.

"I'll make you a deal," my mother said. She was once a reluctant beauty queen. Had once dated Dean of Jan and Dean. "If you wear this dress today, I promise to never make you wear a dress ever again."

She kept her promise, and I spent the rest of my childhood in my older brother's hand-me-downs, corduroy pants rolled up on my ankles, overalls held to my shoulders with brass buttons.

A few years later, after our parents divorced, my brother was walking with his friends, and I followed along behind. He was supposed to see me home safe from school.

"Mandy, are you a lesbian?" he asked, snickering.

I didn't know what that meant, and I don't remember what I answered, but I know all those boys laughed. This is not to demonize my brother. He was infected with the bravado of young boys of the time, showing off for each other.

In middle school, my class waited for our teacher to come to the room and the popular girls talked closely together, pointing at all the other girls in the room in turn. They came to me.

"Hold your hair back," one of them said.

I did.

"Yes. You would be a handsome boy. Not everybody would look good as a boy."

I was strangely pleased and went home to look in the mirror. I scrunched my hair into my palms and hid it behind my head. I wasn't one to stare at myself in mirrors, but I did that day. I never thought of myself as pretty, but I could claim handsome. I would have been a handsome boy.

In high school, I went to visit my father for the summer. He sat across the kitchen table from me, swirling a gin and tonic, in a different Victorian house in Galesburg than the one I had grown up in.

"Do you have a boyfriend?" He paused. "Or a girlfriend?"

I didn't have either, but I could see the searching in him, the man who grew up in conservative small-town Minnesota and moved to conservative small-town Illinois, and what I heard in his question was fear for me, and love. This was in the early 1990s. No one around us was using words like nonbinary or gender identity or questioning. My mind then couldn't even contain the concept of questioning. I had no foundation for it.

Through high school, I wore jeans and t-shirts and leather boots and flannel shirts and tweed jackets like you'd see on a British professor. I didn't own a bra until I was in college. This was also when I began to cut my long hair, hair that would have fallen perfectly in place on a 1960s folk singer. I wanted to look like Keith Richards. I found my physical reflection in music, in men like Mick Jagger and David Bowie, in those moments where they lived in blurred regions, melding genders, looking cool as hell. If I had the knowledge, if I had known the word and the concept of nonbinary then, would I have embraced it? Or would social pressures and my own awkwardness have kept me from it?

The answers to these questions haven't gotten any easier as I've gotten older, and my worldview has expanded. I don't feel fully feminine or fully masculine or even fully nonbinary. I'm some amalgamation of all these things. And so I think of myself as androgynous, a word that for me embraces the ambiguity of both my appearance and my sense of self. I know it's said to be a gender expression rather than a gender identity, but it feels part of the fabric of my personhood. I find comfort in its refusal to draw clear lines. I revel in the space where the ink blurs and smudges.

This is about more than jeans and t-shirts. I've worn my hair short for years, trimming it myself with a razor cutter in front of my bathroom mirror, the tufts floating down around my bare shoulders like falling feathers. For much of my life, I had long, straight hair with no bangs—like my mother always wore hers. Like she still wears hers.

I love my short hair, the epicene ease of it. But I have a recurring dream that morphs in time and place. I'm outside, perhaps standing on a grassy Illinois prairie rise, wind blowing through long hair cascading over my shoulders, like I'm the star of a shampoo commercial. In those dream moments, I feel beautiful. I feel connected to my mother. I wake and worry that I've severed that outward sign of our kinship, our matching hair. But she brings me back to our dress deal from so long ago. She saw me last week, my hair getting shaggy, and she gifted me a haircut from her favorite hairdresser. This is a gift of acceptance; one I have sometimes struggled to extend to myself.

My androgyny has long manifested itself in my writing more by what is absent than by what is present. As I shied away from makeup or skirts or dresses or the color pink, I also evaded my womanhood in my writing while embracing my masculine facets. I wrote about Burlington Northern freight engines and road trips and expansive American landscapes and ghostly memories of childhood in Galesburg and the loss of my father, and then the loss of my stepfather. I rarely wrote about my mother. Never about my body or my dress or the sensation of my shorn locks slipping like satin down my neck.

I have a new project underway. I don't know what to call it. Poems of the body. Poems of the past. Poems of periods, periods of all kinds.

Through this writing, I am reaching inward, looking to explore the sides of myself and my identity that I have not often examined. I am grateful for the ones who came before to light this path, who carried their words in their arms—queer, lesbian, questioning, gay, ace, so many more—and let them float across the world like unquenchable embers.

I still write about trains and childhood and the slipperiness of memory, but now I'm also writing to gather back a splintered part of myself. And perhaps that's the ultimate expression of androgyny in my writing: to broaden my pages, to make room for all aspects of me, and to know they can live and thrive together.

# *Our Daily Walk*
## Christina Lengyel

My husband says the hawk
in the churchyard
is a peregrine falcon. I don't
know if he's right,
and—if he is—when
or where
he learned about birds.
Did I miss that day in the curriculum,
or was it one of the things that changed
in the switchover from Clinton to Bush?
Maybe peregrine
falcons replaced mayflies
in biology class, the same way
abstinence replaced condoms
in health class.

Either way, he seems sure of himself,
so I'll believe him.

Sometimes I hear the bird's cry
from my yard and wonder
if he and his partner might
come take my chickens
or if they are too plump
and vociferous to bother with.
It's anyone's guess
because taking care of chickens
is another thing I didn't learn.
My husband says the hawk
knows we have a dog.
That keeps it away.

Either way, the bird in the churchyard
is some kind of predator.
While walking our bird dog—
who is mostly concerned
with pleasing humans—we all take a pause
to watch the hawk alight
from the ground of the parking lot
to the top of the telephone pole
where he has a view of the whole valley.

I often think about that view,
how it's wasted on the aging
flock of Methodists
who always seem to be inside
if even there at all.

I suppose they've learned
everything they need to learn
from nature—that downward-driving
dove in suspended animation
on the stained-glass window,
that touch-tempting wooly lamb
snuggled so comfortable and close
against a blue-eyed Christ.

Perhaps they've learned
there's nothing more to it all than that.
Or maybe peregrine falcons
are uneasy reminders of earnest
pilgrimages long abandoned
and—of course—death from above.

# *You Were an Apostrophe to Me*
## Ellen Skilton

obscuring the sharpness of divorce debris
and possession's bitter aftertaste, aiding
and abetting painful contractions.

Everything went down so smoothly
at first, and then an acid burn—a shot
of whiskey on an empty stomach.

The perpetual shrinkage triggered
by sounds of angry footsteps on stairs
fueled the salt of heartbreak.

At dusk, I opened the window and tumbled
into an abandoned church lot, the old sign
missing vowels and the dumpster full of vows.

I never liked the hyphen that joined our names
either, but it will never be erased from my CV,
offspring birth certs, my newest mortgage docs.

"You like the things he says," my best friend said in '92.
But an apostrophe can possess with false sounds,
constrain the cruel truth until the sentence ends.

## *Words to Call a Sweater*
### Blaise Allysen Kearsley

The white, chunky cable cardigan you got in second grade was
your favorite, but you never wore it like a sweater. You found that if
you pulled the soft hood just over your forehead, and let the weight
of it, arms and all, fall against your shoulders and down your back,
then you had long, thick, blond hair. Sometimes you visualized
bangs. You realized, resourcefully, that you could tie back the bulk
of the sweater using the long arms to make a low hanging ponytail
or just wrap the arms on top of your head like a half-up, half-down
style. But mostly you wore your hair down. You believed in make-
believe, pretending yourself into something real that you wanted to
see, different from what was there.

You were late for school every day, and your mom late for
work, because combing your wild hair was a harrowing ordeal.
Every morning, a dreaded war to untangle the dry knots and
snags, your head yanked back and snapped forward over and over,
you crying and hollering. When your mom couldn't deal with
it anymore she took you to get your first haircut in a grown-up
salon, where everyone was white like her, and she told them to
cut it all off. Nobody could tell what you were then. (You would
have rather suffered through hair pulling battles in the mornings
if it meant you could have hair that at least grazed the top of your
shoulders.) Once, a girl in your figure skating class glared at your
brown face, your coal eyes, the thatches of black hair poking out of
your crash helmet like she couldn't figure out what she was looking
at. Your name didn't help. Not Elaine or Diana or anything found
on a souvenir mini license plate or flowery ceramic tile. No one
understood what you were saying when you told them you were
called Blaise. "Are you a boy or a girl," the girl sneered, and you
skated off the ice in tears.

Except for at the dinner table when your mom would say, "Take
the sweater off your head, please," you wore it all the time at home,

masking unwieldy, unwanted strands; your calculated over-the-shoulder hair tosses mimicked actresses on TV and in movies, and most of your school friends' signature moves. They loved playing with each other's hair. No one ever asked to play with yours. Even the girls with short cuts had silky, feathered, flippable layers they could run their fingers through. Your hair never moved. A semblance of security lay in the soft cascade that brushed the nape of your neck and the small of your back. The sweater was white, but you called it your yellow sweater. Your secret code for blond.

You started wearing the yellow sweater at school during playtime until one of your white friends asked, "Is that supposed to be your hair?" You'd gotten used to no one saying anything though you always feared that someone would catch on. You dragged your blond hair off your head in front of your friend, and you never wore the yellow sweater in public again. You didn't say anything to her. The puzzle pieces didn't have words, no echo in your voice, no mirror in your name.

****

Some people are really good at puzzles, gravitating to the inestimable pieces spread out on a table. To you, it was all math, and it didn't compute. Too many indecipherable edges. You were like, what are shapes, where do you put them?

Puzzles overwhelmed you and you were irreparably terrible at math. And like combing the snarls in your hair, your mom's help always ended with your hysterics and her anger. There were certain ways in which concepts poured like water into your palms and leaked between your bony fingers. It's just logic, they'd say. You used logic when a teacher asked you on a verbal test how many days are in a week, and you said five. You'd thought to yourself that there are five weekdays and then two days on weekends. She corrected you saying, "How many days are in the week—including the weekend?" You said seven, but you knew five was right, too.

You sensed words by their absence. It seemed like they were sunk at the bottom of the darkened deep end, and no one would dive in, guide you, hold their breath for you to bring the words to the surface. So you kept stepping to the edge to look for them. You waited for the dark to speak your echo.

****

Dad often took black-and-white photographs of you, but there is only one picture you've seen of yourself in the yellow sweater. You'd put it on properly, arms in sleeves, hood flat on your spine. You'd swiped one of Dad's hats, a military camo, the fabric worn on the stiff bill. It was too big for you—perfect for scrunching all your hair underneath, you pressing and tucking the nappy unplaceable pieces that stuck out as best you could. You didn't know that many years into an unimaginable future, you'd finally discover on your own that there was a way to care for your mixed-girl curls, and that they would grow into something you wanted to see. You couldn't have known that the grown-up you, after so much trial and error, would love your hair, and where it came from, and how it became you as much as you once clung to your favorite yellow sweater. You'd love your name, too, and the color of your skin. Soon maybe more things you thought were wrong with you could be right if you let them.

# How Do You Say "No" in Chinese?
Christine C. Hsu


My Belgian boyfriend asked me this question when I was 22.
I paused.
I didn't know.

Yes, I spoke elementary level Mandarin,
But this question stumped me.
Ironically, my white graduate student friend from the
School of Oriental and African Studies
Explained you have to have a verb to go along with the negative.

Bùxiǎng yào - I don't want.
Bù - this "no" doesn't make sense.

The Belgian and I didn't work out.
He wanted a bù.
For me, it was a
Bùxiǎng yào nǐ.

# *Kitchen tales*
## Rina Malagayo Alluri

Despite telling them I do not understand,
they still switch back to Tagalog
I retreat, marveling at their ease
sharing ideas, jokes
amidst stories
of ethnic conflict

Memories of family gatherings,
a name uttered in the kitchen,
incomprehensible sentences,
a punch line,
Titos, Titas, Lolos, Lolas
roar in laughter

We will never know what kitchen tales
have been told about us

When I ask why she never taught me,
she explains I was stubborn,
only responded in English
it is so painful,
a child who did not realize
she was silencing her ancestors

When we fight,
she reminds me
of my linguistic advantage
to formulate rage and frustrations,
extensive accusations
in words I have always known

Angry
she struggles to tell me off in her third tongue

I wonder
how beautiful
it would have been
if we could have yelled
at each other
in Ilocano

# *Are You My Mother?*
## Elizabeth Bowden-David

Every morning from Bangalore, with my first sip of cappuccino, I call my mother in Memphis to wish her good night and sweet dreams. The phone rings for a while. My brother, who is now her caretaker, says she fumbles to retrieve her cell phone and fiddles to push the right button. Occasionally, the line disconnects before she succeeds, so I dial back. Each exchange essentially repeats the one before. Illness has stolen most of her memory—for example, she doesn't recall that I've lived in India for the last dozen or so years—but has left her Southern sweetness perfectly intact.

"Hey Mother! I just called to hear your voice. Hope it's not too late."

"Aa-OH no, no, no. I'm just sitting here counting my blessings."

After that, I might tell her an amusing story or what I cooked for breakfast.

"Today I fixed buckwheat pancakes with roasted strawberries for the boys."

"Ahhh, you're creative."

"Nah, I just followed a recipe."

"Well, you're making memories."

Now and then she loses the thread of the conversation. Still, she punctuates with her favorite phrases and sayings:

> If you see someone without a smile, give 'em one of your own.
> A person wrapped up in himself makes a small package.
> You're a good mother.

I don't get to see her very often nowadays. And I regret that she hasn't seen my life in India. She'll never witness how the glass tiles in my roof filter the moonlight, decorating my floor and walls with bright, dancing rectangles. She'll never hear the rhythmic thwack . . . thwack . . . thwack of my boys swinging the cricket bat against the practice ball that hangs outside on a long string. She'll never watch parrots flitting among the sunset-colored blooms of a Flame of the Forest tree.

But the undeniable truth is that she and I are nothing alike. My father and I, people said, were two peas in a pod. He passed away when I was 21, the same year I left Alabama. A nine-month study abroad program in Germany turned into a four-year stay across Europe, by the end of which I realized my fascination with the great wide world was no passing fancy. I moved to Arizona to earn a master's in international business and then skipped off to Asia when the ink on my degree was barely dry. Aside from a stint in California (which most of my kin consider foreign anyway), I've been outside the U.S. ever since. Part of me acknowledges that had my father lived longer, I probably would have missed him too much to stay gone. Yet for all my adult life, I've forgiven myself for residing thousands of miles away from my mother.

P.D. Eastman's *Are You My Mother?*, the adorable tale of a baby bird who—when his mama is away—hatches, tumbles out of the nest, and totters about searching for her, was my favorite storybook as a child; my mama bird read it to me until the binding frayed. As I grew, the question went sort of underground in my soul, as in "Is she really my mother?" How could I have sprung forth from this woman from whom I am so very different?

She really is the sweetest person anyone knows. She did try to teach me, but it hasn't always stuck. Once, when she was visiting me in Singapore, as we rode in the back of a taxi and I pointed out features of the city skyline, she jabbed my ribs with her elbow. I wracked my brain to figure out what she was trying to tell me. She jabbed again, glanced in the direction of the driver (who was in the middle of a coughing fit), then glanced at my purse. I had no idea. Finally, in gentle exasperation she whispered, "You have mints in your purse. Offer!"

On the same trip she met my husband's aunt, whom we had gotten to know well over the previous year. I had told my mother all about her. Yet within a couple of hours of their introduction,

it was my mother who seemed to be more in the know. As they
sat knee-to-knee on the sofa, my husband's aunt poured out
deeply buried stories we had never dreamed: how she actually was
a mother of four, not of two as we believed. She had lost one baby
a few days after his birth and another when he was six months old.
We had no idea.

My mother always thinks of people, above all. When I was
living in Europe, I showed her Munich and Prague; she cared little
for the towering cathedrals and cobblestone streets, but for years
afterward fondly recalled the train ride between the two cities,
because that's when we had a warm conversation with a pleasant
Englishman. When I was living in San Diego, she flew in for
the delivery of my first baby and stayed to help ease me into the
routines of motherhood—and within one day of her arrival was
on a first-name basis with the checkout clerk at the local grocery
store. I had been shopping there for a year and knew none of the
employees. When I first moved to India and learned that I had
to tip the postman to guarantee delivery of my mail, she couldn't
understand why I didn't find out his name. By contrast, the day
before her own postman retired, she surprised him by filling her
mailbox with a basket of candies (sugar-free, she explained to me,
because she knew he had diabetes). That has always amazed
me: Our home was in an over-the-mountain Birmingham suburb—
not some fictional small town like Maycomb or Mayberry—so
exactly how does one get to know a postman?

Even in her illness, she still has that extraordinary quality about
her. Two years ago, when I was visiting her in an assisted living
home, I called an upholstery cleaner to spruce up the La-Z-Boy
in which she was spending most of her waking hours. The young
man arrived when my mother was out getting her hair done. I was
polite enough, I suppose, but was preoccupied on my laptop. Yet
within half an hour of my mother's return, he had opened up to her
about his drug addiction and his gratitude for a Buddhist-inspired
treatment program, his tender hope about a girl he had started

dating, and his worry about not having much to offer.

✶✶✶✶

For all my mother's sweetness, it bothered me early on that she didn't seem to jump into life the way I wanted to. She didn't swim because she didn't like to get her head wet. She always turned the radio down. She would fret endlessly about getting a thank-you note just right, her pen swirling in invisible, halting circles above the card before she was confident enough to ink the words. It was this nagging sense of otherness that prompted me to say the meanest thing in my life. I was about seven, and she was putting me to bed. I looked her full in the face.

"When I grow up, I'm not going to be like you."

What she felt, I don't know. But her reaction was all grace and lightness.

"That's alright. You can just be your own person. I wouldn't want you to be like me anyway."

She kissed me goodnight and never mentioned it again.

In defense of my seven-year-old self, what I probably meant was that I would do things she hasn't. This has come true. I have a career. I scuba dive. I throw parties. I bench press. By exaggerating a teeny bit, I can say I have faced down a hissing cobra. I dance in the kitchen. I occasionally cuss in front of the kids. When someone tells me good news, I jump up and down and whoop and holler with unbridled glee.

Today, I'm the age she was when I was a teenager. If I ever expected the years to narrow our differences, they have not. The enduring question has morphed from "Are You My Mother?" to "Is she really my mother?" and now to "Where is my mother?" Aside from our daily phone chats, where do I see her in this life I have built? Not only that, where does she really dwell at this moment now that illness seems to be nudging her slowly but surely into the spirit world?

My father has been on the other side for decades now, but his presence feels nearly constant. So where is my mother's influence?

There's a little indentation in the nail of my index finger and darn it if it isn't just like hers; I get an odd feeling when I hold the emery board. There's a certain laugh that mimics the rhythm and resonance of hers; last weekend I heard it after a guest told an entertaining tale, and it left me with a queer feeling that I had borrowed a voice. But there's no mistaking the driving forces of my life for hers. When I look in the mirror of my actions, I squint, but she's nowhere to be seen.

I've been pondering this question for years, and the answer that feels truest is rooted in my very first memory of life. I am about four or five. I am standing in front of the TV, wearing an Auburn jersey and Toughskins jeans from Sears. Caught off guard, I feel the rustle of something being dropped into my back pockets. When I rush my hands backward into the denim, I find that each pocket holds a piece of Super Bubble. I whip around, but the treasure-giver has concealed herself behind my back. I delight at holding the red, yellow, and blue-wrapped morsels in my palms, while I hear my mother's gentle chuckle behind my ears.

I suppose that's still where she is, where she has always been— and that's why I don't see her in the mirror. She's not inside me or around me but behind me. She holds my back straight with her unconditional acceptance, and she propels me forward with a sense of freedom to be my own self. I can crane my neck around to try to see her, but really, there's no need. Just like the day she slipped treasures into my pockets, she has ducked out of view. She is right behind me, too close to see.

# Escape Velocity
## Wren Donovan


She knew me well-enough to know that I would lose her.
She smiles beside a road somewhere. Polaroid hills
are faded grey, her breast is white, her large eyes sharp and dark.

She conquered gravity by only willing
escape velocity at her command.
Earthbound, I watched her wheeling arc curve wider every time,
     her shadow on the sun receding smaller with each pass, elastic
          inhale then exceed across a field of space behind my half-closed
               mammal eyes until
          movement all dissolved in empty blueness.
Now I am condemned to watch the sky.
I do my time and wait for feathered shapes against the light.

From a photo edged in white her eyes still hold me.
On the back I read my name in girlish loops.
She knew me well-enough to know
that I would need a souvenir. Memento flutters, joins the flock
of paper memories in a box. A fragile click of chain turns out the light.
Old muscles slide the heavy door and lift my skull to scan the sky.
She knew me well-enough to know I wouldn't fly.

# *Will They Know?*
Janet M. Powers

Tourists, is it, swarming the coast,
gobbling the mountains in two days,
Welsh appendage to a tour of Britain;
or the English, coming on holiday,
swallowing whole the last bit
of land they never could subdue,
hordes of them, buying love spoons,
to say they've been there, seen
the inside of yet another siop.

Will people know I am different,
if I come on foot, with few pennies,
softly, as a lover comes in tryst?
Wanting not so much great castles
as meadows full of buttercups,
worn villages tucked into valleys,
menhirs to dance around; embracing
the rain that feeds the grass and oaks
standing tall with their druid wraiths.

I'll come quiet with remembrance
of forests ravaged for the iron furnace
and earth raped for coal seams within.
Leaping centuries, I'll come, genes in
hand, molding the hollows of my spirit
to the hills of Cymru, the spikes
of my anger softened by the tender
vowels of Cymraeg, 'til I sleep green
and wondrous in the cradle of her arms.

## *Sightseer*
### Kari Ann Martindale

Bedouin in the sky,
the ephemeral wanderer drifts
from terminal to terminal,
photographing plane wings
and food trays
and backpacks stowed beneath.

Caravans of affluence trade tales
under the veil of enlightenment
en voyage
to raid cultures for selfies.

# Glasshouse Mountains
## Kathryn Reese

> The storm bird cries all summer,
> never when it rains.
> Avian omens cannot be trusted.

I take the range road, the coast splayed out to my left, scented with roadside
lantana, mango, and open sclerophyll sweat. Mt. Coolum gathers clouds like
a skirt, come lie here, place your hand on my rock chest. The Maroochy gives
herself to the sea. I trace her shimmering, seeking the mangrove-lined bend
my grandfather fished, the footbridge picnic island, our great-grandfather's
farm now marked by a concrete pylon that lifts a motorway over the river.

> Maroochy:
> lover's tears.

> I belong to her
> estuarine
> embrace,

> her
> curves,
> her salty
> mouth.

> I leave her sandy kisses in my tangled
> hair dream dark
> mangrove arms
> to reach,
> caress her grief.

Humidity laced with lantana. This scent, this forest. My blood. Generations
of hollow giants, axe-scarred, filled with mushroom, moss, loam. Wonga
vines secure canopy to earth with long, loose stitches. Creek mud seeps,
sleeps beneath the impending storm. Sacred water. Sacred air, slung with
mosquito heat.

> We felled the forest to find
> no rich soil,
> only dust.

> Tibrogargan weeps.
> His name has been restored
> but not his land.

# *They need to invent a Korean word for adoptee sorrow*
Maria S. Picone



*after Franny Choi's "Hangul Abecedarian"*

Gather up all us thousands
Negated,
Disenfranchised from greater han
Like an embarrassing family
Member stashed in a Western country
But macro—
Scale of oceans rise
-ing, masticating sovereign shore,
Journeying back to our livable land.
Check our feelings on a Likert Scale
Korea, home language we watered down
To flood the wider world, now
Pushing back against the carbon-fired
History we're burning from.

# *Amanecer/Anochecer (from Dawn to Dusk)*
### Elaine Elinson

**Amanecer**

There is never a thick fog or dark cloud to a Chiquila dawn.
The half-carved valley takes only light to paint its sunrise. The
surrounding green mountains guard their choices.

Sometimes it is purple silver. A light mist captures the blue and
diffuses it into lavender shades through the corners of adobe rooms
and slits in orange tejas. The mist whispers that this day, a light
rain will fall, feathery and silent, approaching from an unnamed
distance. And if it is this way, just as the sun rises the world
turns purple.

Other days, the dawn is gold and green. The sun strews golden
drops where the leaves of the higo tree brush white adobe walls,
where silver rocks break the current of the river, where children
splash and play. These golden mornings promise days of a heat
that make the trees in the distance so clear you can count their
branches, a day bathed in yellow sparkling light.

And sometimes—if you wake just as the sun is bringing
Chiquila to life—there is a mosaic of all the colors, purple, blue,
and golden green. You walk early in joy and mystery. These are
rare dawns with quiet colors like the underside of the rocks that
lie on the shore of the river, and outspoken colors like the reds and
oranges and greens that arch above it. Your soul gently gives itself
up to let the colors decide what kind of day it will be.

**Mediodía**

A rooster crows, but not for the first time. A rooster crowed
last night at midnight when the sky was aglow with stars and early
this morning when sunrise was fading into daylight. And as he
crows now, the hot sun makes the stones in the dusty dirt road
shimmer with heat. The rooster crowing does not mean dawn
here unless dawn is to be felt at all hours. That, as with so many

symbols, does not follow the rules here. Rooster is rooster and will crow at will. He will set the rhythm of the country, the background music against which the marimbas will play, the machetes will swing at stalks of sugar cane, water will be drawn from the river for drinking, strong hands will shape the masa and slap tortillas on the comal.

With a crack, the sky opens and fat round raindrops splash on the broad banana leaves. The rain starts in the middle of the sun, shadowing the blue sky to black and gray, splattering loudly. Then suddenly it disappears, leaving only puddles in the rutted street for toddlers to jump in and mangy dogs to bathe.

### Anochecer

The fading sunlight hits the pear-shaped wooden curves of the guitar. Don Chico's fingers fly in and out of the sun, only making music, not noticing the patterns they make on the panel of the wood worn thin by decades of strumming. Faded cornflower-blue pants cover his long spider legs, crossed one knee over the other. A frayed straw hat is drawn over his dark eyes, casting a shadow over his gaunt cheekbones and black mustache. Muscles in his neck, like strong ropes, quiver as he croons.

The boys head home from the milpas, stop for a swim in the river, wrestle, and catch fireflies. Reaching their house, they grab a tamal sin pollo, kiss their mama, and gather around Don Chico. Eliberto, Orlando, and Manuel don't really know if they are still boys or if they are men. They barely notice the dusky sky, slowly filling with pale stars, or their mother lighting the lantern. They tap their feet to the cumbia and listen to their fathers talk of soldiers and crops.

# *Still Loading*
## Hana Worku

Please wait a minute // this page is still loading // Addis Ababa 2016

While I'm cooking food in a pot for dinner
a high-rise building is approved for construction
a neighbor sits on a plastic stool watching television

While I'm sitting in a side alley computer lab waiting for Facebook to load
a friend's cousin steals her passport
an old man guards an unmarked office door

While I'm combing my hair in the mornings
a gas shortage starts and then stops and then starts again
a Chinese worker arrives at the Addis Ababa airport
a giant hippopotamus swims in a polluted lake

While I'm waiting in line at the bank
a church and mosque compete with loudspeakers for prayers
a boy shines leather shoes under an old umbrella

While I am sitting in the middle seat of a van
squished in place by other passengers, boney hips
the driver looks at me through the rearview mirror
smirks, and asks "lemedesh . . . lemedesh ende?"

I know the question well. A verb, meaning
are you comfortable? Are you well adjusted?

These verbs are a problem
when telling time is a problem
when, at least grammatically speaking,
the present is continuous

"I'm eating"
before you have even picked up a plate
"I'm coming, I'm on the way"
standing by the window and watching the rain fall

That's why when they ask me, "lemedesh," I respond,
"iya lemedku new"
progressive tense

Yes, I'm getting comfortable,
I'm getting somewhere
I'm starting to understand
I'm adjusting
I'm figuring it out

# *The Essayist Reaches for Poetry*
## Tamiko Nimura

for Audre Lorde

**First Position**

I was too brown, too round for ballet as a child. Pink slippers,
not-me-nude tights. Always reaching away from ground. The Y
teacher told my mom, "Weak ankles."
I stopped. Wrote my first haiku.

**Second Position**

Essays, though, they say what you mean. Essays say, throw words
around. Maybe away. Clear your throat in an interesting way. State
your thesis, or your question. Same thing. Then try, just try, to answer.
Five paragraphs, please, double-spaced. You know the
form: dutiful, college-ruled.
Isn't it easier?

All my acrobatics transferred to the water.

**Third Position**

Poetry says, oh, but I'm swimming.
I've got the flip turn.
Check out my agility!
Love my flexibility!

Poetry barely ever
comes up for air.
Here, look for me, it says,
Reach out.
Research.
Reach me.
Tosses its hair,
then it's gone.

**Fourth Position**
I never learned the flip turn.
OK. Fine. Now I can learn.

Kiss your knees.
Forward flip.
Maybe use a nose clip.

Don't flip
        all the way!
Then, stretch out.
        Touch the wall.
Not too high, not too low.
        Now, kick off.

It takes practice.
        Learn it in an hour.
It takes practice.
        Reach.

**Fifth Position**
Reach again,
        see the world
        upside down.

Let the water hold you
        as you cut it
        with your hands,
        your legs.

Reach again. Dance with
        bright blue
        freedom before you.

# *Runaway Poem*
## Jen Gayda Gupta

Do you think we've beaten the system here?
Just us and the dog, soaking in a new side of the sun.
Mornings you carry me from bed, no coffee, like exhaustion
can't find us here, safe from the migraines and serrated
commutes and never mind the WiFi connection tethering us
to cash source, never mind when I ask strangers, "doesn't everyone
hate their job a little?" and can't tell if they want to laugh
or cry. Here in this little cottage, with its honey-tipped trees
and cricket conversation and never mind the punctuation
of bullets, deer thudding to the ground, because we can just stay
inside this house, with its mosaic mountain view, and watch
the rainfall. Because we can leave when we get bored, settle
into a new countryside, maybe even a city. We can pretend
we are not aging. We can lower the sounds on our meetings,
satiate our skin in the middle of the day. Remember that weekend
in Lake George? I don't need to go in to detail and never mind
that it was us. Everyone has had a Lake George back in their beginning.
Why is Lake George always back in the beginning? I know
exactly what we're running from, but I don't know if it will catch us.
Friends keep texting me pictures of themselves, teeth bared waving
a pregnancy test in front of their face. And never mind
the way I reach for my stomach every time just to make sure
it's still flat. And never mind the way I sometimes push it out,
make myself a little bloated belly just to convince myself
I don't like the way it feels. Everyone wants to know when
this will stop and wouldn't I like to tell them.

# *Flight of the Nightingale*
## Oanh Nguyen

The meaning of my name
is Flying Nightingale.
I took flight to flee
far away from home

without a map
or compass
or even destination.
I step off a plane
in America.

A terrifying landscape of
white snow suffocating streets.
I drift along
in this cold, sterile world.

Thoughts, feelings, memories
are vague fearful shapes
where no one knows my name
in a post-apocalyptic land.

Every day the teacher
taps her chest: "Mrs. Brown."
Then she taps my chest
and names me "Teresa."

I stare at her searching
for words and understanding.
Mrs. Brown shakes her head
and sighs "How peculiar!"

My body wanders.
My mind engages.
Yet I am trapped
in a cage.

In the dark bedroom,
I mouth the words.
"Phi Oanh" . . . I tap my chest,
"My name is Phi Oanh."

# *The Hawk*
## Diann Leo-Omine

I spy:

> a hawk on the levee, splayed out on harsh gravel.
> Who would hunt a bird of prey
> who was bold enough to take down a raptor?

> In Latin, raptare means "to seize and carry off"

The day she returned from the hospital I called her on FaceTime. She was almost more lively than I'd seen her in the last five years. Alzheimer's had otherwise frayed the mind of the grandmother I remembered from my childhood. Out of nowhere, she rattled off a roll call of our names in the village dialect, in a pitch so clarion no one could afford to be tardy.

This is how I want to remember her.

****

Because of pandemic-related restrictions, no visitors were allowed at the hospital. Yet almost no staff could communicate with her since they didn't speak Toisanese—except when she cussed out the doctor. By admission of her feistiness, they deemed her well enough to go home.

> Raptare: to seize

Days later, despite the new lease on life her hospital stay infused her with, she had a bad fall that sent her back, a fall that took both the moon and sun out of her.

I visited her when she returned home. That astonishing clarion from earlier in the week had disappeared. I knew as I walked down the steps of the house that I would never see her again, as much as I selfishly hoped that she could stay to greet my child's birth.

> Raptare: to carry off

After the visit, as the weaving of ghostly fog and rapid sunshine brought the cherry blossoms early, a hexagon of pink etched itself into the near-twilight sky. A grim and gritty optimism I needed to remember; to remind myself that I could survive hard times, that there was beauty even in the harshest moments, I took a photo.

****

Insiders and outsiders, loved ones and curious strangers (Chinese and not), wonder why I don't speak my family's language. They don't mean to be accusatory, but it grates on me when they ask:
"Why don't you speak your family's language?"
"Don't you want to learn?"
"No one will call you that name again because your language is dying, even in the motherland."

Do you die along with it?

Raptare: to seize

Our names are in a dialect no one will call out again, names I can't bear to hear again unless it's from my grandmother or my grandfather. It's not as simple as learning or not learning so much as it is untangling the murky ocean that is trauma.
In my wandering year traveling Europe and Asia in 2018, I found myself triggered by the extended question: If I spoke the language or not, what was I doing, a woman, a woman of color, traveling alone, hiking with expat strangers who were not my husband?

Raptare: to carry off

There is a photo where you can see I am crying but I do not face the camera. For once in my life, there was no need for language. I will see the place I am from. I will feel the place I am from. I will arrive.

56

I wouldn't be the first person to grieve in a language I didn't understand.

****

I spy:

> a hawk perching on her porch.
> Brows growing inward
> the hawk glares with promise.

Talons digging into prey, the hawk tears its rodent dinner apart in view of my grandmother's kitchen pantry.

Sometimes, the hawk makes a return. The hawk comes, the hawk goes. I give the hawk an absurd name. I then ask my child, now a toddler, if he wants to see the hawk when it comes for a visit. I want to ask the hawk where it's been and why it keeps returning.

There are different meanings applied to hawk sightings, but many I've seen suggest a hawk sighting is liberation, a vibration of higher awareness, awakening, anew. I don't dig any deeper, but for now pocket this newfound freedom like a stone. It just may have been a gift from her.

Raptare: to seize and carry off

# *Roaming.*
## Patricia Falkenburg

no one needs

where we should
stay

to tell
us
us
stay

adrift

on the wings

of a hummingbird hawkmoth
in midair
to stay

humming audibly and
no place

hovering
in midair

where we should

trust

come or go

on our own

wings only

hovering and humming
good omen

they said

even in the rain

even in the rain

flight
over waste
or

bounty
by visual discrimination
by convergent evolution

settled unsettled

reached unreached

the endless
the flight

ending
endless
floating
flying

always
floating
away

no one needs
and

we are

us
peregrine

# *On the Cover: Shey*
## Daryle Newman

mixed media analogue collage and acrylic on paper

She is a being who transcends any one-dimensional codification of woman.
She has lived a thousand lives and through a thousand labels.
She will no longer be told who she should be or ask permission.
She will break the rules enforced upon her.
She is unapologetic.
She is nature, power, intelligence, and technology.
She is peace.

Art is the tool I use to navigate and take back my female body, my sexuality, and my function free from the constraints of reality. I allow my process to be fluid, meaning once begun it takes on a life of its own within my head and hands until it presents itself to me. An artwork initially created as a visual response to a particular climate crisis, for example, might often transition through my thoughts on childhood trauma, lived experiences, or research then circle back through compositional choices and mark-making, to become a visceral embodiment of a hybrid creature whose job it is to be an environmental caretaker, a conscious warrior, or consequence of neglect instead. My art is my freedom to be a reclamation of self and an homage to the many that I admire.

# Contributors

**Rina Malagayo Alluri** was born in Mumbai, India, to a Filipina mother and Indian father, raised in Nigeria, and migrated to Turtle Island (Canada). She currently lives in Austria, where she is Assistant Professor in Peace and Conflict Studies at the University of Innsbruck. She is cofounder of The BIPOC Circle, an initiative that holds space and place for BIPOC people. Her poetry explores (de)coloniality, identity, and relationships that form/unform. She is a yoga practitioner, soul searcher, and mama to two headstrong children.

**Elizabeth Bowden-David** is Alabindian . . . at least that's what her husband calls her. She grew up in Birmingham, Alabama, hopped and skipped across a few continents, and now lives in Bangalore, India. As a recent empty nester, Elizabeth is rediscovering the adventure of new beginnings—including using the written word to honor the people in her life.

**Rebecca Brock's** work appears/will appear in *The Threepenny Review, CALYX, Mom Egg Review, Rust + Moth, Whale Road Review*, and elsewhere. She won the 2022 Muriel Craft Bailey Memorial Poetry Contest at *The Comstock Review*, judged by Ellen Bass, and the 2022 Editor's Choice Award at *Sheila-Na-Gig*. Her first chapbook, *Each Bearing Out*, is available from Kelsay Books. She is a reader at *SWWIM*. You can find more of her work at rebeccabrock.org.

**Wren Donovan's** poetry appears in *Harpy Hybrid Review, Moist Poetry, Green Ink Poetry, Emerge Literary Journal, Anti-Heroin Chic*, and elsewhere in print and online. Two chapbooks are forthcoming: one inspired by myth and fairy tales, the second on themes of embodiment, brokenness, and remains/remaining. She studied Classics, literature, folklore, anthropology, and psychology at Millsaps College, UNC-Chapel Hill, and the University of Southern Mississippi. Wren also reads Tarot, practices dance meditation, and talks to cats. She lives in Tennessee.

**Elaine Elinson** is the coauthor of *Wherever There's a Fight: How Runaway Slaves, Suffragists, Immigrants, Strikers, and Poets Shaped Civil Liberties in California*, which received a gold medal from the California Book Awards and a starred review from *Publishers Weekly*. A former reporter with Pacific News Service, her writing has appeared in the *San Francisco Chronicle*, *The Nation*, *Woman's Day*, and other publications. She was awarded residencies at Hedgebrook, Mesa Refuge, and Ragdale and was named a San Francisco Public Library Laureate. Her earlier book, *Development Debacle: The World Bank in the Philippines*, was banned by the Marcos regime.

**Dr. Patricia Falkenburg** is a molecular biologist, poet writing in German and English, and visual artist. Born in Mannheim, she currently lives in Pulheim near Cologne. Her poems have been published in numerous anthologies, journals, and blogs. *Portugiesische Notizen* (Portuguese notes) was published in 2019 as LyrikHeft 24 with Sonnenberg-Presse, Chemnitz. She loves to collaborate with artists of other fields—currently a goldsmith, musicians, painters, a photographer and conceptual artist, and graphic artists. She is a member of several German author groups, notably the GEDOK (Cologne).

**Jen Gayda Gupta** lives, writes, and travels in a tiny camper with her husband and their dog. Her work has been published or is forthcoming in *One Art*, *Rattle*, *Sky Island Journal*, *Up The Staircase*, *The Shore*, and others. You can find her on Twitter @jengaydagupta and jengaydagupta.com.

**Raychelle Heath** holds a BA in languages from Winthrop University and an MFA in poetry from the University of South Carolina. She uses her poetry and her podcast to tell the multifaceted stories of black women in the world. Raychelle also explores her experiences with the culturally rich communities that she has encountered in her travels. Her work has been published by *Travel Noire*, *Fourth Wave*, *Yellow Arrow Journal*, *The Brazen Collective*, and *Community Building Art Works*. She currently works as curriculum director, sanctuary coach, and facilitator for the Unicorn Authors Club. She also regularly facilitates for The World We Want workshop.

**Christine C. Hsu** is a poet, playwright, and essayist based in San Francisco, California. She has been published by *The Bold Italic, xoJane, KQED, ABC News Radio Online, Livina Press, Lunchbox Moments, Slipform Poetry Anthology 2020, Mixed Mag, DropOut Literary Magazine, NonBinary Review, Nonwhite and Woman Anthology, Red Ogre Review,* and *Soft Star Magazine.* Her plays have been performed by the Negro Ensemble Company, Crafton Hills College, Houston Community College - Stafford, The Pear Theatre, Enterwine, and The Playwrights' Center of San Francisco. The Writers Grotto of San Francisco selected her as a 2022 Rooted and Written Fellow for Screenplay.

**Blaise Allysen Kearsley** is a Brooklyn-based Black-biracial writer and teacher and the creator/producer/host of *How I Learned*, a long-running storytelling, comedy, and reading series. Her writing has appeared in *Catapult, Longreads, VICE, The Boston Globe, Midnight Breakfast*, Electric Literature's *The Nervous Breakdown, Oldster*, Elle.com, three creative nonfiction anthologies—*Nonwhite and Woman* (Woodhall Press, 2022), *Cringe* (Crown Publishing, 2008), and *Mortified: Real Words. Real People. Real Pathetic.* (Gallery Books, 2006). She teaches creative nonfiction writing for Gotham Writers Workshop, 7 Daughters of Eve Theatre & Performance Co., Writing Workshops, and Blaise Writers Workshop, which she founded in 2017. She is currently a contributing editor at *Vestal Review*, the oldest flash fiction journal on the planet.

**Amanda Kooser** (she/they) is a freelance journalist and longtime contributor to CNET specializing in goofy rocks on Mars. They graduated from the University of New Mexico creative writing MFA program in 2022. Their work has appeared in the *Harwood Anthology* and *Conceptions Southwest* with upcoming pieces in *The Twin Bill* and *New Mexico Poetry Anthology*. Amanda cruises Route 66 in Albuquerque in a pink-and-chrome '50s car and plays a pink-sparkle guitar in the indie rock band The Dawn Hotel.

**Christina Lengyel** is a writer and performer. Her work is most often fiction that accidentally feels like poetry and rarely goes anywhere in particular. She has a bend toward the mystical and is often a bit creepy. She completed her MFA in creative writing and publishing arts from the University of Baltimore with a few credits from the Jack Kerouac School of Disembodied Poetics at Naropa University. Christina is the editor of the central Pennsylvania-based site, *Raven Rabbit Ram*, and host of the podcast, *It's Always Saturn*.

**Diann Leo-Omine** (she/her) was born and raised in San Francisco, California (Ramaytush Ohlone land), and the colorfully boisterous Toisanese diaspora. She now resides in California's North Central Valley (Nisenan land) between the ocean and the mountains. She was awarded a 2022 creative nonfiction fellowship with Rooted and Written at the San Francisco Writers Grotto. She cocurated and edited the Asian American food zine *Lunchbox Moments*. Her writing can be found in *The Six Fifty*, *The Universal Asian*, *Write Now! SF Bay's Essential Truths*, and the BIPOC Writing Party's forthcoming anthology.

**Kari Ann Martindale** has been published in various literary journals and featured in festivals, ekphrastic events, and literature nights across Maryland. She sits on the Board of Maryland Writers' Association, helped get EC Poetry & Prose off the ground, and holds an MA in linguistics. Her poem "The List" was a finalist for *Line of Advance's* Colonel Darron L. Wright Award. A globetrotter at heart, she's always planning her next trip. She prioritizes kindness over politeness and justice over peace.

**Daryle Newman** brings with her a mixture of storytelling and adventure. As a mixed media artist, her art is indicative of the interconnectedness between the natural world, feminism, science, climate change, philosophy, politics, and the metaphysical realm to depict the spaces between. Her practice questions her own and humanity's effects on the Earth and each other, their ignorance or indifference to make changes, and their triumphs and uniqueness, alongside her belief that beneath habit and conditioning, there is always a desire to be and do better and that women must be their own and each other's champions. Daryle spent several years overseas in the Republic of the Marshall Islands cofounding an arts NGO, returning to Australia to formalize her passion for the arts industry by completing a Masters of Curating and Cultural Leadership at UNSW Art and Design in 2020. Daryle has since worked at multiple art galleries and NFP creative industries in Sydney, Australia, and continues to hone her own art practice. Her most recent art is a layering of fact and fantasy about the power of the female to be changemakers, both in the realms we understand as real life and in other worlds in which she seeks guidance, contemplation, or distraction. Ultimately, her art celebrates unrepeatable moments by honoring unrepeatable females.

**Oanh Nguyen** was born in Vietnam and emigrated to the U.S. with her family in 1975. She is currently a part-time online student at the University of Pennsylvania, focusing on creative writing. She currently lives in the Philadelphia suburbs with her daughters and other animals. Her work appears in *Poet's Choice*, Sad Girl's Literary blog, and *Herstry*.

**Tamiko Nimura** is an award-winning Asian American creative nonfiction writer and public historian living in Tacoma, Washington. Her words have appeared in *Off Assignment*, *The Rumpus*, *Modern Loss*, and *Full Grown People*. She is a regular columnist for Discover Nikkei, a web project of the Japanese American National Museum. She is working on a memoir titled *Pilgrimage: A Japanese American Daughter's Reckoning With Memory and History*.

**Ray Oldham** is a queer, disabled writer who spends her day-to-day working at a florist and navigating a life with chronic pain. She attended UMBC for her bachelor's degree in English literature, and she hopes to continue her education in a graduate program for writing and editing. In her free time, she enjoys reading, watching reruns of *Love Island*, painting her nails, hanging out with her cats, and creating entirely too many Spotify playlists. She's looking forward to her 27th birthday, adopting more plants, and spending as much time with friends as possible.

**Maria S. Picone/수영** is a queer Korean American adoptee who won *Cream City Review's* 2020 Summer Poetry Prize. Her debut chapbook, *Adoptee Song*, will be published in late 2022. She has been published in *Tahoma Literary Review*, *The Seventh Wave*, *Fractured Lit*, and more, including *Best Small Fictions 2021*. Her work has been supported by The Juniper Institute, Palm Beach Poetry Festival, Lighthouse Writers Workshop, *GrubStreet*, *Kenyon Review*, and Tin House. She is *Chestnut Review's* managing editor, *Hanok Review's* poetry editor, and *Uncharted Mag's* associate editor. Find out more at mariaspicone.com or on Twitter @mspicone.

**Janet M. Powers**, Professor Emerita at Gettysburg College, has published poetry in many small journals. Her chapbook, *Difficult to Subdue as the Wind*, appeared in 2009. This old lady still stands with signs on street corners hoping to make sense of our sorry world.

**Leticia Priebe Rocha** received her bachelor's from Tufts University, where she was awarded the 2020 Academy of American Poets University & College Poetry Prize. Born in São Paulo, Brazil, she immigrated to Miami, Florida, at the age of nine and currently resides in the Greater Boston area. Her work has been published in *Rattle*, Roi Fainéant Press, *Overheard Lit*, and elsewhere.

**Kathryn Reese** is a writer and poet living in Adelaide, Australia. She is passionate about the collaborative process and facilitates workshops that assist participants to settle anxiety and access creativity. Her writing explores themes of nature, spirituality, myth, and the possibility of shape shift. She has published a small poetry collection, *Despair Dragon: notes on survival*, and her work will appear in Neo Perennial Press' forthcoming *Heroines Anthology* (released November 2022).

**Laura Rockhold** is a poet and visual artist living in Minnesota. She is the inventor of the golden root poetic form and is working on her first collection of poetry and a multidisciplinary art exhibition that explores the interconnectedness of environmental and social issues and healing. Her work appears in *Black Fox Literary Magazine*, *The Dillydoun Review*, *The Hopper*, *Quail Bell Magazine*, *swifts & slows*, *Variety Pack*, and *Yellow Arrow Journal*. She holds a BS in child psychology from the University of Minnesota. Find her at laurarockhold.com.

**Ellen Skilton** is a professor of education whose creative writing has appeared in *The Dewdrop*, Cathexis Northwest Press, *Quartet*, *The Scapegoat Review*, *Dissident Voice*, *Philadelphia Stories*, *kerning*, *Red Eft Review*, and *The Dillydoun Review*. In addition to being a poet, she is an educational anthropologist, an applied linguist, and a Fringe Fest performer. She has an MFA in creative writing from Arcadia University and lives in Philadelphia, Pennsylvania.

**Hana Worku** is a writer, software developer, and organizer interested in how things are put together. How do things work and why do they work this way?

www.ingramcontent.com/pod-product-compliance
Lightning Source LLC
Chambersburg PA
CBHW031549310726
48971CB00008B/2688